FOR ALL

D0634362

FOR ALL THAT IS OUR LIFE

A Meditation Anthology

HELEN AND EUGENE PICKETT
EDITORS

SKINNER HOUSE BOOKS
BOSTON

Printed in Canada.

ISBN 1-55896-496-7
978-1-55896-496-9

Library of Congress Cataloging-in-Publication Data

For all that is our life : a meditation anthology / Helen and Eugene
    Pickett, editors.
        p. cm.
    ISBN 1-55896-496-7 (alk. paper)
    1. Spirituality—Unitarian Universalist churches. 2. Meditations.
    3. Prayers. 4. Poetry. I. Pickett, Eugene, 1925- II. Pickett, Helen
    (Helen R.)
BX9855.F67 2005
242–dc22   2005009029

CONTENTS

We express our liberal religious identity in our contemplation as well as through our action. The writings in this anthology are largely personal. They speak in a wide variety of voices, represent various theological points of view, and are written in different styles and forms—poetry as well as prose. All of them give expression to the familiar hymn, "For all that is our life we sing our thanks and praise," bringing a delightful harmony to the range of expression and symbolizes the unity in diversity so central to our liberal religious faith.

Meditating is a means for focusing our attention. The object of our attention can vary widely—from God to nature to silence—but the desired goal is to increase our awareness, to help us realize that we are part of something larger than ourselves, to help us deepen our sense of relatedness. Meditation can also help call to mind some forgotten or neglected aspect of our own life. So in a sense, these meditations written by others may call to our attention reminders of ourselves and invite us to explore them further on our own so that we may gain a better perspective on our whole lives, on our being and on our doing.

We have been greatly impressed by the volume and variety of responses to the request for material for this anthology. For these aspirations, meditations, and prayers, and "for all that is our life," we too give our thanks and praise.

Helen and Eugene Pickett

FOR ALL THAT IS OUR LIFE

In the quiet sanctuary, the choir paused for a moment. The lovely silence of sacred Sunday morning struck me as I meditated upon the mysteries of our shared human existence. Out of the calming quiet, the soft music began its melody and the choir's voices joined. They sang, "For all that is our life, we sing our thanks and praise."

My soul seems caught up in those words. Somehow, for everything, I can give thanks. Even the painful moments must have their part. I feel a deep sense of gratitude for all of existence. Yet I find myself asking, *is it real?* Perhaps not, but I am moved to think that perhaps religion might mean acceptance, gratitude, compassion, and forgiveness.

For all that is our life, we sing our thanks and praise.

For joys that ignite our passion for life, and for suffering borne so that life may continue, we sing our thanks and praise.

For human closeness that warms us, and for the distance that reminds us to turn away from our hatred and impatient disrespecting, we sing our thanks and praise.

For forgiveness that heals our separations, and even for repentance, which is nothing but the humility to

acknowledge our faults and flaws and which allows
and leads to self-transformation, we sing our thanks
and praise.

For caring,
for love,
for the call to give one's self,
for the joyous, silent song in our inward being,

for all that is our life,

we sing our thanks and praise.

HENRY SIMOKI-WASTILA

ORDINARY GRACES

The red orange glaze on the low-sunk moon
seen in the parting of clouds.

The sight and sound of a bright field of wheat,
whispering, bending in waves.

The scent of a windborne sea, pine, jasmine,
and the waiting gifts of a harvest table.

The gentle tug of creation's umbilical cord
calling us out of despair.

The warmth of linked hands and shared thoughts,
calling us into community.

These gifts of grace we receive.
In them we rejoice
as we return our thanks.

JOY ATKINSON

DIVINITY

It comes to me when I am most creative,
when I am thinking things
and doing things
that reach beyond myself
—not knowing,
only hoping, dreaming—
wanting revelations to connect,
support and nourish.
And when the energy
surges up and lifts me
toward the light
into space
where sparks ignite
and inspiration crackles
from the brain into the heart and back,
then everything around me sings.
The spirit speaks and lives
and I am filled with wonder
at the beauty of this place

we call the world.
My gratitude knows no bounds.
My life is full,
and I am blessed beyond
all sense of self or separateness.
I am the world and all
that is within it,
and I bless the holy grace
by which all lives.

DOROTHY BOROUSH

THE BLESSINGS OF COMMUNITY

Alone in the world, I was beset with frustration and anger at the world around me—so much injustice and hatred, so little peace and freedom. I longed to make a difference, I struggled against powers and institutions. But my actions seemed insignificant and my words were drowned out.

Then I came into community, a religious community of hope and love. Here I found support and energy, vision and power, the authority of shared witness.

And together we changed the world.

Alone in the world, I was beset by sorrow and hurt in my life—so much loss and emptiness, so little hope and understanding. I wept for the pain in my heart. I ached from the hardships I bore. But my tears brought little relief and my burdens grew too heavy.

Then I came into community, a religious community of hope and love. Here I found support and compassion, wisdom and grace, and the power of shared suffering.

And together we made life sweeter.

Alone in the world, I was beset by confusion and emptiness in my soul—so much busyness and pettiness, so little depth or connection. I shriveled inside from want of real spiritual bonds and my soul cried out for meaning.

Then I came into community, a religious community of hope and love. Here I found support and encouragement, depth and diversity, and the power of sharing the journey.

And together we saved my life.

For all the varied reasons that have brought us out of loneliness and into community, we give thanks. For the blessings we each bestow on one another with our energy, compassion, and prayer, we give thanks. For the blessings we become to others in need, we give thanks and remember that we are not alone.

DOUGLAS TAYLOR

BLUE AND GREEN IN SEPTEMBER

September afternoon, the back yard:

The sun still high enough in the autumn blue to drop her golden rays over the top branches of the dogwood, landing warm on my back. A breeze comes and goes in cycles, rustling the leaves. Stately oak, maple, and ash trees stand in full foliage, robustly green. The two giant arborvitae continue to amaze my eyes with dazzling yellow-green tips, each gently waving like hand-held Japanese fans. Things are overgrown everywhere I look, silently screaming for attention, for weeding, pruning, thinning, and mowing.

Not today. Today, I'm listening to September.

Birds seem quiet or missing, their song replaced by insect chatter and bees. One buzzing at my arm flies off for places unknown, most likely to the color in the neighbor's yard. A bright pink hibiscus the size of a dinner plate peeks over the split rail fence from behind tall ornamental grasses. Beyond that I see the bright orange-yellow of marigolds, geranium red, and scores of budded mums. I dream of a well-groomed yard, a masterpiece, with properly trimmed trees and shrubs, a wider expanse of lawn, and a rock and water garden. I'll put it nestled up against the stockade fence—a place where birds and butterflies will congregate, spending time among favorite flower foods.

Not today. Today, I'm noticing September.

Our dog Parker is browsing around, nose to the ground, exploring, sniffing, stopping to roll on his back, bearing his full weight into some irresistible scent. He's twisting and pushing himself about with his feet, making pleasure noises. He stands up, shakes off, and goes down again for another turn, pressing his muzzle against the grass, fully responding to what calls his attention at the moment. I think I should roll in the grass again—be more in the moment as I was when I was a child. I remember how much fun it was to lie on the lawn and look up at white clouds parading across the great blue sky in shapes of flowers or bunny rabbits, wild horses or scores of mythical creatures.

Today, I'm aware of September.

No clouds float overhead. It's pure blue, sustaining and endless. I look skyward; directly overhead are the undersides of elm leaves, some nearly transparent with sunlight, gold and green flesh between the structure of veins, others dark in the shadows. I remember how much I loved blue and green together. Then I hear my grandmother's voice ringing clear across time. She'd say, "Blue and green should never be seen," whenever she saw me wearing those two colors together. Didn't she ever look up at the sky through the trees on a clear September afternoon and notice the perfection? If she were here today, I would show her what she missed.

CHRISTINE LEWIS BROWN

OF COURSE

Of course I want the truth,
but here's the rub:

Truth doesn't sit around
still as a rock,

it breathes and flows
and turns inside out.

Ever seen a lion in a cage?
He paces and glowers.

That must be how God feels
locked in our little religions.

Look how big the sky is,
the deep distances between stars.

Little speck, that's you;
laughable speck, that's me.

How could we contain The Truth,
all that overwhelming light?

Our truth is just a pinprick
in mystery's velvet curtain.

Even so, see how we struggle
to fix an eyeball to that—

peepshow's tiny window.

JANET HUTCHINSON

I AM A MILLIONS-OF-YEARS-OLD WONDER

I am a millions-of-years-old wonder.

I am an international—no, cosmic—treasure.

I ought to be safeguarded in a museum somewhere like Paganini's old violin. I ought to be gasped
at, talked about in hushed, amazed, reverential
tones. Viewers would touch me gently and feel lucky.

Daily newspaper headlines could say, "Mary Feagan
Exists Again Today!" Radio and TV shows could dis-
cuss me, my ordinary events—that I saw a bluebird
with my millions-of-years-old eyes and heard it sing
with my highly advanced, evolutionary ears; that my
graceful hands with opposable thumbs fed my sensi-
tive mouth delicious strawberries that it tasted.

Then without a conscious thought, my brilliant
brain directed my masterful, complex digestive
system to assimilate and use them for fuel to wash
dishes, write poems, hold babies, laugh, and give
kisses.

No one would completely understand or dare to finally say how my marvelous, magical, famous, fine self exists, really.

I am just, bottom line, a millions-of-years-old-wonder. You are too.

MARY FEAGAN

THOUGHTS WHILE PICKING RASPBERRIES

City people make assumptions:
that there will be food at the store,
that the air conditioning will come on when wanted,
that the earth will keep spinning,
keep looking blue and green from space,
keep making life.
So that's why I pick raspberries,
celebrate each broccoli crown,
eat fried green tomatoes,
crawl around looking for cucumbers,
bend double over pea vines,
thin carrots,
weed turnips,
collect varieties of squash.
I don't want to assume—
I want to care.

SARA JONSBERG

EQUIDISTANT

The center of the universe is in this small room
where our souls touch the infinite,
and grace surpasses all our understanding.

And the center of the universe is in the nest outside
the window where the tiny speckled eggs are about
to hatch under the watch of attentive parents.

And the center of the universe is held by the young
mother in the bus going past as she cradles her new-
born in her arms and wonders where her future lies.

But the center of the universe is also in the heart of
the bomb crater where bits of bone, and chair, and
cup are all that remain.

And the center of the universe is also in the jug of
water carried by the small boy walking past the
garbage heap where his brothers search for their
day's sustenance.

And the center of the universe is also in the quiver-
ing salmon just caught and eaten by the grizzly bear
in the cold Alaskan stream.

And the true center of the universe is millions of
light years distant from an insignificant solar system
in an average galaxy that some call the Milky Way.

May the consciousness of the universe that connects

all souls comfort and strengthen each one and
bring peace and wisdom to every life.

JEAN M. OLSON

MY SONS

Sometimes my sons are Children of the Sun,
intense and radiant,
excited and streaming with energy.

Sometimes my sons are Children of the Stars,
steady and ever-present,
independent and limitless.

Sometimes my sons are Children of the Moon,
cool and distant,
not avoiding but not reaching out.

Sometimes my sons are Children of Venus,
affectionate and loving,
close and considerate.

Sometimes my sons are Children of Mars,
defiant and challenging,
determined and strong-willed.

Sometimes my sons are Children of Jupiter,
deep and mysterious,
dramatic and powerful.

Sometimes my sons are Children of Saturn,
beautiful and creative,
delicate and fragile.

Sometimes my sons are Children of the Comet,
wandering,
curious, investigating.

Sometimes my sons are Children of the Meteor,
suddenly chaotic,
violent and majestic.

My sons are Children of the Earth,
solid and grounded,
resilient and self-confident,
Children of Creation.

KIT LUEDER

A FREE AND RESPONSIBLE FOSSIL HUNT

On a hot Monday in July, my family went out hunting for dinosaur fossils. This was an activity that Keenan, our middle child, had requested for his birthday party. Keenan turned ten years old back in April, but there had been some delays. If we had been able, for example, to coordinate sooner with the paleontologist who took us on the tour, we might not have been so hot. We invited five families to join us and we explored two different sites. We drank a lot of water that day. (Did I mention that it was very hot?)

As it turns out, Washington D.C. sits atop a fossil band that runs parallel to the eastern coast. Our paleontologist guide told us that this is a crucial point: If you are going to try to find dinosaur fossils you should look where you can reasonably expect to be able to find some. We did not find any fossilized dinosaur bones. We found sharks' teeth, crystals, very old rocks, and also petrified wood from the time of the dinosaurs. Our paleontologist guide told us that this is a second crucial point: If you do not find anything it does not mean you lack special skills or have not tried hard enough, it just means you have not been lucky enough.

Our religious lives can be like searching for dinosaur fossils on a hot Monday in July. If you are going to try to find religious nourishment, you would do well to look where you can reasonably expect to find some. For example, read the Tao Te Ching, the Bible, and the Humanist Manifesto, go to church, join a covenant group, increase the amount you give to charity, sing in the choir, volunteer to help people in need. These are tried and true places where one can reasonably expect to find religious nourishment. And if nothing special happens, or only happens for you once in a long time, that does not mean you "don't get it," or you're not trying hard enough. It simply means you have hit a dry time in your spiritual life. Remember that this can still be a wonderful time if you don't worry and you don't stop reading, attending, singing, and serving as you usually do. Trust also that the dry time will end and you will find that fossil or be struck by that deep personal and spiritual insight. And it never hurts to drink lots of cold water.

DOUGLAS TAYLOR

AGNOSTIC

Give me where to stand
and Archimedes' pole,
and I will churn Earth's stagnant waters,
and pry her into new orbit
away from Moses, Mohammed, Christ, and all
to a sweep ten-thousand Milky Ways across,
where God is not form, or Earth-words—
neither legislator nor accountant,
but resident physicist and gatekeeper
of the last black hole.

JACK LANDER

THE YUCCA

The yucca grows content,
accepting its charge with fervor.
Rugged green, spiking skyward,
unbending, unyielding, undying.

Sending forth the seeds of itself
to mature within majestic clusters,
offering the white blooms
to Her Majesty and the bees.

The flowers fade, die, and drop away.
But the very life of the yucca remains in
the wooden replicas of its offerings,
in a grand statement of fertility.

The pods dry out and pop open,
spilling black seeds of acceptance
to the earth in abundant glory. There
is hope of renewal again and again.

The yucca grows content,
without negotiation or questioning,
without seeking approval,
but with acceptance of its purpose.

CHRISTINE LEWIS BROWN

FIRST DAY OF SCHOOL

No matter what they tell you,
let it be about joy
let it be about the sacred
self surviving—no, thriving—
shining its way to the knowledge within.
Let it be about blooming,
the unfolding of the universe through you,
because the story of you begins
fifteen billion years ago
with that first flash of being.

At four, you reached out your hand
into the dark night and pulled
back in wonder, a firefly blinking
from your finger. Keep that magic,
that both you and the firefly are one,
everything connected,
everything possible,
made of stardust and moonshine as
we all are.
Let it always be
about
your shining.

NITA PENFOLD

THE BLUE CHINESE BOWL

Mother owned a blue and white Chinese bowl
    so large it might have held mountains
    of sharp-crowned pineapples, sunrise peaches,
        ripe pears.
It might have held bunches of roses, pink, ivory,
    flowing over its sides, dropping petals on the
        table.
Perhaps it was full enough with stories of the
Colonel's wife,
    her estate watched by Grandpa, her gardens
        fragrant.
White porcelain elegantly brushed with blue
chrysanthemums,
    perhaps this bowl needed nothing.

When mother got divorced she ran quickly from
our small house,
    leaving her china but she took the bowl,
    and as I grew she said, "Someday it will be yours."
In ugly houses warped with rage
    it opened serenely.
When I was grown and she moved again, she sold it.
    "Why?" I screamed. "You promised."
    But she couldn't say.
The bowl has stuck in memory,
    hard with anger.

Mother's gone, the question discarded
   with many others.
Now I give away anger, blue chrysanthemums,
   falling petals.

LEONE SCANLON

CREATIVE SLOW DOWN

For me, creativity is an act of slowing down. Paying
attention. Taking time. Never doing in one day
what could be spread out over seven, including a
day of rest. It is no coincidence that this is also how
I meet the divine.

But this can be difficult. It is so easy to fill life to
the edges, to the brim, to the darkest corners of
early morning and late night too, until there are no
remainders. Running from one commitment to
another, adding tasks between appointments,
returning calls between tasks, wedging things too
big into times too small, a half hour here, ten minutes there, or a second right now. Just a second, I
might say, borrowing time from one need to address
another. There is no time to create something new.

A book artist friend of mine once told me the
beauty of her art form is that it cannot be done in a
hurry. Like the stepping stones in a Japanese gar-

den, intentionally placed to slow our pace, almost any creative act will, in some way, require that we stop hurrying a painting laid down in careful strokes, a meal thoughtfully prepared in an afternoon, a quilt lovingly stitched over weeks or months, or a book written over the span of years. Both the making and the enjoyment of creative works require that we take our time. "Poetry is about slowing down," Mark Strand once said. "You sit and you read something, you read it again, and it reveals itself a little bit more, and things come to light you never predicted."

Creative living is full of encounters with the unpredicted. Divine surprises. Revelations that will take your breath away, and give it back again, time and time again.

My need for creativity reminds me to slow down—to pay attention to the unpredicted, to take the time to write a poem, to take the time to read one. This is how things come to light for me. By taking time, and sometimes repeating things. Never doing in one day what could be spread out over seven, including a day of rest. It is no coincidence that this is also how I meet the divine.

KAREN HERING

CONVERSATIONS

The dirt road, dust spilling
over car windows, the view that I
craved for over a year,
opens to encompass what the
mind has held all winter and through
the mud and black flies of spring.

Slowly I back the car toward
the side door, watch the last
of the dust settle, and sit;
home is so far away, I am alone.
The stillness now, at full summer,
hurts.

The screen door has not lost
its peculiar complaint, the
inside door still sticks at
the threshold, a shove
and the room accepts me
in its benign, aloof indifference.

Hello house, in my loudest voice.
No response. In each room it is the same.
The furnishings, glad for the release
from winter's stiff hold, have relaxed
into their summer creases and wrinkles.
Curtains billow like angels in flight.

No more toys under the beds,
no piles of books and clothes
spilling out of backpacks,
the beds are made and will stay
that way, no requests for lights
to stay on or one more drink of water.

I put lights on in their rooms,
one light in every room,
for me this time, because
I can't stand the dark. I talk
to the house because the silence,
where laughter lived, aches.

The conversation with the house continues,
questions to the lighted rooms go
unanswered. Where have the years
gone to live and why did they take
so much of what I loved with them?
Insects and bats fly against the screen.
Night.

I listen for little feet
seeking the big bed and one
more story, hear only the rustling
in the lilac. Talk to me, house,
tell me I said yes. I am here if anyone
needs me. Good night, everybody.

JACQUELINE BEAUREGARD

MEMORIAL SERVICE

They will go on, without their mother,
the two girls she left.
Their father will go on,
lonely in the house they had shared.
Her mother's eyes fill
as she speaks of how old she is herself,
how ready to go at a moment's notice,
and here she is, incredulous,
sitting by her daughter's ashes.
Life is definitely out of order.

It will not do
to speak to them of a divine plan,
or to say it's for the best.
It is an insult to suggest
her life was
somehow complete,
and besides, it's just not true.

We will remember her together,
and speak of happy times,
and weep that those times
are from a story that ended
before anyone was ready.

MARY WELLEMEYER

PSALM IN SIX STAGES

Oh, Eternal One,
Great God of Power and Might,
Redeemer, Savior, Carrier of Light and Love,
I am indebted to you for your steadfast faith.
I had only missed you for a moment but I feared it
    was to be a lifetime.
You are indeed masterful and at ease.
Alluring Cosmos, Universe, Great Mystery,
I am humbled by the unfolding tapestry of life that
    once begun has never ceased.
I am in awe of the small human mind that seeks to
    unravel your secrets.
In one moment we grasp the complexity, then it is
    gone.
For all the sages have said is true,
and all the artists have imagined is real.
The Way is revealed, the One is here.
Experience tells us that there is only love.
In this moment at the tip of time that is now,
Great Wondrous Goddess, Spirit, Energy of
    Creation,
may I continue to be humbled by life's beauty and
    finitude,
may I feel its magnitude and sense immortality in its
    everlasting flow,

may I work for justice as a beacon of compassion for
an ocean of seekers.
May my life be a prayer with the reverence for all
that lives.
We are all worthy of this precious gift given to us at
birth.

Blessed be and Amen.

JOANNE GIANNINO

COULD IT BE

Could it be, Holy God, that your loving spirit, your
caring, your eternally benign creativity and deep
parenting affection for me also wash me of all guilt?
Am I—for all my faults and failures—beautiful in
your sight? Feeling your presence this way, my God,
restores me to innocence and hope, even for
myself, for my salvation and human success. I am
full of failure and regret, I feel inadequate and
blameworthy, yet I do feel you love me profoundly
and completely, and that conviction lightens my
heart and creates in me a new self. Speak to my
heart every hour, mysterious spirit friend, so I may
feel re-made and renewed in vitality, in surrender to

things as they are around me, and graced within by
this healing sense of your presence. May it be so.

WILLIAM CLEARY

ON BEING THE MOTHER OF AN ACTIVIST

I am writing "apples" on my store list.
My daughter is in jail.
I am hanging the wash on a line as a clean breeze
    tries to tug it out of my hands.
My daughter is in jail. Is she frightened?
I am swimming in the river with my children, feel-
    ing the current pull at me, watching the flash of
    small silver fish gliding around my legs.
My daughter is in jail. How long will they keep her there?
    Is she able to take a shower?
I am sitting in a darkened theater with my best
    friend, watching her son sing and dance upon
    the stage, stealing glances at her face as it lights
    with pride and love.
My daughter is in jail. Why is she doing this? With the
    simple saying of her name she could be free, but she
    chooses to stand firm and remain, and so my fear for
    her remains, imprisoned within my skull, beating on
    the bars.

I lie in bed, unable to sleep, unable to stop the
    whirl of anxious thoughts, pinned by the terrify-
    ing images of angry policemen's faces, barely
    restrained cops in riot gear, stark cells.
My daughter is in jail. Can she sleep?
I am jolted awake at midnight by the shrill cry of
    the telephone. Is she finally able to call us?
My daughter is in jail.

TESS STARECHESKI

HIGH ON HOPE

There is during the worship thing at our church
a piece called meditation.
We are all quiet.
Well, not perfectly quiet, no.
Charlie's stomach grumbles behind blue denim,
Martha's little Jennifer fidgets and scrapes her feet,
Dale coughs and stirs and his wife pokes a lemon
    drop in his hand.
It's a fabric of sound impossible not to hear,
utterly without intention or sense or rhythm,
but quiet is what we mean to be.
These are long minutes
to be so communally alone!
I always have the goal of moving inward

and finding focus
and catching glimpses of meaning and purpose and
    wholeness,
and sometimes—not often—I do.
I collect these moments
to hoard them back at my place.
If I save enough of them,
I think, they'll start to look and feel and comfort
like peace
or union with the ultimate
or some such thing that's really good and grand!

JACK KING

CALLING

I take deep pleasure in quiet moments when in the
distance I hear the mournful calling of ship's horns.
My childhood was framed with the early-morning
and late-night sounding of train whistles, low and
long in the silence.

Ever since, in each place I've lived, there have
been trains to sing their slow songs like whales
crooning in the deep. But here there are no trains.
There are boats that haunt the night with extended
exhalation. It might be a law of physics: Humans
must hear long, low calling in the dark.

Do boats and trains evoke the wind moaning through canyons, when the Anasazi waked at night to listen and wonder? The storms sweeping across the Serengeti? The groaning and cracking of the earth, the organ pipes of deep caverns playing their songs long before humanity woke to paint pictures on their walls?

Far from trains and boats and whalesong there is a deeper, longer song the universe sings to itself. We all are in it. If we listen with our hearts we can hear it, the voice of Life and the longing of all living things.

JENNIFER BROOKS

TO SAIL A BOAT

To sail a boat requires a sharp and constant awareness of the elements. One must be aware of the winds and tides, directions and landmarks, shoals and hazards, the dangers of a sudden storm or the risk of finding oneself becalmed. It requires a sense of yourself, how you interact with the boat, and the elements of nature.

With time and patience and experience, you can integrate what you have been told and taught with what you sense and feel to produce a sort of wisdom. As you sail, you draw on this wisdom, as well as conscious awareness, to guide your actions.

The wise sailor knows that he or she cannot oppose or ignore the forces of nature. You learn very quickly that you cannot sail directly into the wind. But with careful tacking, you are able to get to your destination. Most of all you learn that at all times the satisfaction is in the sailing, well done and fully experienced.

With experience you learn to recognize that there are times to stay in harbor, just as there are times when the call of the wind and water are not to be resisted. You learn to welcome the difficult times, which test every ounce of wisdom and muscle, just as you welcome the hours of smooth sailing with its lazy relaxation.

You develop a sense of awe and respect for the raw and brutal power lying in the forces of nature. You know that you are not master of these powers, but with respect and careful apprenticeship you may be allowed a sort of limited partnership.

You never lose your sense of the sublime beauty that surrounds you and touches your cheek with the wind-blown spray.

As it is with sailing, so it may be with all of life. As it is for the sailor, so may it be for me, for you, for each and every one of us.

PAUL L'HERROU

HUMMING TO SNAILS

What did you do on summer vacation? Our children have been answering this question all week in classrooms all over the city, but I'm afraid no one will ask me. So I've decided to tell you anyway. I learned to hum to snails.

On a lazy Sunday afternoon in July, I sat with my ten-year-old cousin on the rocky shore of the Damariscotta River in Maine. I watched as he patiently held a snail that he had plucked from the rocks—and hummed to it! I didn't know whom to watch, the boy or the snail, but soon I saw two antennae appear from the shell and the snail began to dance! Of course, I had to try it. It wasn't long before all the other adults had moved from the porch down to the rocks, each one holding a snail and humming to it. A dance troupe of snails!

Two things struck me about the experience. One was the quiet power of that youngster in teaching us something about our world. He didn't tell us anything but allowed us to discover it for ourselves. We forgot our adult anxieties about looking silly and abandoned ourselves to humming.

The other was in the form of a theological question. Is there something out there in the universe humming for us to come out of our shells, urging us to dance? Trying to understand what moves us is one of the reasons we come together in a religious community.

MARJORIE SKWIRE

A SEASON OF GLAD GIVING

In the winter season of holidays, we occupy ourselves with many traditions of giving. Our gifts may be boxed and wrapped, tied in bows and ribbons, laid under trees, or delivered one day at a time. In our many different ways, we participate in this generous giving and grateful receiving, exchanging gifts of time and music as well as material blessings. Yet sometimes, in the flurry of all the holiday exchanges, it is easy to lose sight of the real meaning of this glad giving.

For on any day, in any season, a gift is no small thing. Given in gladness and without expectations, a gift is an opening of the heart, an offering of one's self, an exchange of love, respect, or good will, or all of these at once. Even the simplest of gifts— sometimes especially the simplest—can be a powerful thing. As Jon Kabat-Zinn writes, "At the deepest level, there is no giver, no gift, and no recipient . . . only the universe rearranging itself."

In the traditions of many tribal cultures around the world, a gift is something that must, by its nature, keep moving. The person who receives a gift is often expected in time to return it to the one who gave it, give it to someone else, or pass on a different gift in its place. The important thing is to keep the gift moving in the larger sense. A gift held too tightly ceases to be a gift.

As we consider the many gifts we've been given over our lifetimes—the talents we received at birth or by training, the circumstances and opportunities that have blessed and shaped us, the comforts we enjoy materially, emotionally, and spiritually—we might ask ourselves how we will keep these gifts moving.

Perhaps this is the reason for the old tradition of writing New Year's resolutions so soon after the gift-giving traditions of December. It may be the best time for remembering, with gratitude of heart, all that we have been given and considering, with generosity of spirit, all that we might give back. It may be the best time to understand how we might participate all year long in the radical and restorative rearrangement of the universe.

As we move through this season of giving, let us be grateful for all that we receive and let us remember to keep our gifts moving.

KAREN HERING

DYING OF THIRST

"Near Vast Bodies of Water, Land Lies Parched"
New York Times, *August 12, 2001*

Lake Michigan is receding:
what was marsh last year,
full of cattails, loud with frogs,
is caked and dry this year.
Fissures of worry and waste run jagged
through the baked mud.
Water will be more precious than oil,
the man said.
The day draws near
when even luscious lands like ours
will be dry-mouthed and panting.
New England was built on its water power.
Imagine it with none.
Imagine Seattle with no rain.
Imagine the frail-skinned bubble, Earth,
with no blue,
no swirling clouds of white.
Imagine an apocalypse of tongues
dragged between teeth,
crazy for a cool splash of just one drop.

SARA JONSBERG

IS THERE TIME?

It's not that Death is fearsome,
though the manner of dying
can turn thoughts gray.
It's not to put off death
for its own sake, for fear of it—
this carefulness with eating,
this exercising,
these vitamin capsules
that might be needed or not—

no, it is a love of today,
of being alive.
There's so much to do
and such passion for doing—
this sunrise,
the flowers of that tree,
the touch of this hand,
the words of that friend,
this work to do,
these paths to walk.

No, I'm afraid of running out of time.
Let death not come too soon,
but in the fullness of years,
at the end of a long adventure of
unfolding, blooming, as never before.
And just in case,

let me rest in each day
and cherish each moment.

MARY WELLEMEYER

CYCLING

On a warm December day
I edge toward sixty years
and take to the woods to clear
my magpie mind and find
some comfort in the play
of light on leaves.

The gaunt old trees
without their summer canopies
flaunt each naked gnarl.
Some have branches, even trunks, ensnarled
in vines so thick they've grown to ripeness twined
like loving-chafing mates
or stalwart Jobs empowered by ordeal
and blessing their fates.

Like a low-hung floodlight in the wing of a stage
where dancers make their meaning out of shapes,
the winter-solstice sun illuminates
a ballet of decaying landscapes.

The leaves heaped on the trail
do not crackle underfoot or scatter
like ancient bones when shattered.
Now past the rustle of October,
past the rainstorms of November,
they labor quietly, seeking their natural bliss,
intent on their moist metamorphosis.

Nothing of growing green to be seen.

Yet everywhere—from blinding west to golden east,
clogging streams, filling hollows, padding slopes,
leaves glisten, their muted palette a motley feast
in hues of spices, gourds, and roots,
in shades of nuts and grains and fruits:
of almond, chestnut, saffron, ginger, russet,
tawny onion, squash, and claret beet,
of bosc pear and nutmeg, yam and fig,
of pumpkin, cinnamon, and honeyed wheat.

And over all, in every molecule of this warm air,
the humid, pungent smell is rife,
exciting to inhale—
the strong, assuring scent of surging life.

PATRICIA MONTLEY

I DO NOT HAVE CHILDREN

I do not have a child, but if I did, I would teach that child wisdom. I would protect him and make sure he knew how to protect himself. I would nudge her toward high ideals and plenty of resilience. I would tell stories of my life—both happy and sad ones—and the things I learned. I would remind him things don't always work out perfectly—that mistakes happen. Success and joy are usually found by improving on our failures and then finding ways to let them go.

I do not have a child, but if I did, I would probably feel paralyzed at times with the magnitude of my responsibility. Knowing that the time we're together is short compared to the list of lessons to be learned. I would be overwhelmed knowing that there will never be a moment when my child is not learning something and that, in the long run, he will remember me, good or bad, as one of the most important teachers he ever had. I am sure I would live with uncertainty, wondering if I were doing the right thing or enough of what was needed. I would try to not push too hard, but hard enough to let her know how much I care. I would not want to be his therapist but I would want to be someone with whom he could share his problems. I would feel the anguish of knowing I could never completely cure her dis-ease with life's dilemmas and incongruities. I might not even understand her dis-ease, but I'd be resigned to suffer it alongside her for the time we're together, hoping my support will help her even after I am gone.

I do not have a child, but if I did, I imagine the hard part would be figuring out how to get the light into all the dark places she is apt to wander—not knowing how often, or how long, she will feel at home in the glow of my adoration. The hard part would be remembering the pain of my own past and hoping I have found ways to let healing—and not hurt—shine from those memories. The hard part would be the mixture of fear and hope. Fear that I will eventually fail to protect her from hurts and pain and that she would be miserable if I somehow succeeded. Hope that when the world does test her, she will stand up and shine. And I guess, having a child would mean a good deal of prayer. Prayer that one day my child will come back to me beaming with joy, explaining how he has made the world a brighter place and how the world made him a brighter person.

I do not have a child, but I know that this is neither a reason nor an excuse for new generations to go without my experience, my vision, or my care. I do not have to have my own children to love what children bring to this world, to help them, hold them, inspire them, and make them capable of living on the level of their dreams.

I can teach. As long as I have beliefs infused with truth and love and a place to act out my beliefs, I can make a difference. And in so doing, I have many children. And I have a legacy. I can change the world.

GREG WARD

FIRST SNOW

Snow sifts from pale sky
lacing leaf and branch.

A squirrel acrobats
up a crabapple tree
along the highest, thinnest limbs—
unbending despite its weight—
disturbing not a flake of settled snow
along a single twig.

That I might live that way:
seeing all my world
whole
from such a height
of quiet, yet
not bending any branch
nor displacing snow,
only tasting air, bounding,
pausing, poised.

Or at least this way,
in gratitude from where I sit
before the single candle flame,
watching through the window—
squirrel, branches,
falling snow.

KAREN LEWIS FOLEY

RESPONSIVE PRAYER FOR CHRISTMAS EVE

In this season of sacred hymns and rousing carols,
how can we keep from singing?

Spirit of Life, remind us to sing.

In this season of celebrations and joy, when there is
still plenty of loneliness and despair behind the tin-
sel, how can we keep from caring?

Spirit of Life, remind us to care.

In this season of miracles, when a bright red ribbon
of mystery is wrapped around this gift we call life,
how can we keep from wondering?

Spirit of Life, remind us to wonder.

In this season of anticipation and magic, when children's faces beam like Northern lights, how can we
keep from laughing?

Spirit of Life, remind us to laugh.

In this season of hope, when people throughout the world are praying for peace and goodwill, how can we keep from praying?

Spirit of Life, remind us to pray.

And in this season of darkness and candlelight, when the flame is passed lovingly among us in fellowship, how can we keep from shining?

Spirit of Life, please keep our candles lit throughout the coming year, and remind us to shine.

Amen.

ROBIN L. ZUCKER

DAFFODILS WAKING

At the height of the siege of cold and snow, rain and flooding, a warning sign—like those that say "Children at Play" or "Cattle Crossing"—was posted on Westford Street, just a little way up from the church. It said, "Daffodils Waking!"

Well, who would have guessed? I hadn't even seen green shoots. But someone, whoever designed and posted that sign by the road, was going on faith. Someone was hoping against the evidence that somewhere under the earth, the daffodil bulbs were still there and starting to wake up. Someone noticed the light was staying longer on the earth and the birds had new notes in their songs. Someone said to him or herself, "I'm going to spread a little hope among the folks with whom I share this corner of the earth."

The letter to the Hebrews in the Bible says, "Now faith is the assurance of things hoped for, the conviction of things not seen." Assurance. Conviction. These are very strong words. Things hoped for but not seen. That's what faith does in us. It goes against the evidence. It hopes—not as in "I hope it won't rain on our picnic," but as in "I hope we'll find a way to balance the budget" or "I hope human beings undergo a change in consciousness that brings about a more just and merciful existence for all beings."

Hope seems to me the growing edge of faith. It is what makes us keep on keeping on. It makes us go forward against evidence, even against failure. It makes us take our feet out of bed each morning and put them on the floor even after a sleepless night of worry and no evidence that things will be better tomorrow. Hoping against evidence keeps us alive—moving, working, praying, giving ourselves to the human enterprise.

I am sure daffodils are waking.

KAREN LEWIS FOLEY

PATIENCE

After the burnished day,
    when the sun burrows out of sight
    behind the first ridge of the Front Range,
    pulling the light of sky behind him,
    a great patience descends
    upon the shadowing land.

The mountains with their crests of rock or tree
    stand quietly and wait.

The fields lie still and wait.

The animals graze silently or wander toward their
    shelters.

The clouds, still bright against the sky,
hang motionless or drift with slow deliberation
toward the dark.

The earth that bustled through the pressing hours
    since dawn
        takes up an age-long vigil.

It has waited out primordial fires.
It has waited while continents rose and sank
    and wandered through the seas.
It has waited for wind and water
    to round the ruptures of its crust
    into slopes and curves

of the sensuous body of the Great Mother,
    ever ancient, ever young.
She has waited for her children and their going out.
She has waited for her lovers and their drawing
    together.
She has waited for their homecoming at the last.

The night will come, with its panoply of stars
    whose secret stories are her own.

Underneath, the earth will wait.
In the morning, she will still be there.

WALTER ROYAL JONES

YOU, GOD, ARE THE WAVES

I am the beach,
and you, God, are the waves
that lap against my shores,
washing over me completely.
You are always present,
loving this sand and body
you have created.
Your day child,
the sun,
warms me.
Your night child,

the moon,
illumines my evenings.
Your breezy child,
the wind,
caresses, and at times
rearranges me,
as nature and life
have a tendency to do.
No matter what my condition—
smooth, glistening,
disheveled, or muddied—
I am never without Your Presence, God.
I am the beach,
and you are the eternal waves that
lap against my shores.

RITA COLEMAN

THE GREAT BLUE

The haunting remains of a hardwood forest hold
some thirty great blue heron nests above the
spreading depths of a beaver pond. When the fog
moves across this swampy rookery everything, even
time, is suspended in mystery.

It was a timeless childhood moment when I saw
my first great blue land. It descended through the
trees onto the waters of the meandering stream

behind my home. It came down quickly with knobby leg landing gear horizontally stretched out behind. Slightly above the tall nettles on the far bank it pulled them abruptly vertical and landed on the soft bank across from a giant beech tree. Having effortlessly accomplished this feat, it projected a sense of the eternal as it kneaded the mud and began fishing. The landing of a pterodactyl could not have done more to freeze the motion of time. Moments passed and then the big bird awkwardly rose in flight along the path of the stream until it was out of sight.

No other creature linked to my childhood can take me so swiftly into timeless awe and wonder. I hunger now for such suspended moments when time is irrelevant, age meaningless, and every creature a natural link to the eternal.

STEPHEN SHICK

REMEMBER PEACE

Fear, impatience, anger,
resentment, doubt, greed,
you are welcome here.

We will hold you until you soften.
We will love you until you begin to melt.

We will sing to you until you remember peace.

Darkness and sadness,
loneliness and sorrow,
come.
You are welcome here.

JILL-BETH SWEENEY SCHULTHEIS

SOLSTICE

Her last days were beautiful and spare—
bare limbs corkscrewed into sky,
claret and burgundy leaves,
the world backlit
as everything fell away,
shape of the hills a clear rhythm.
She pointed at December.
A sparrow lit on the unexploded cattail
in a cluster of stalks.
Brown suede split
releasing a fluffy salvo of potential:
lightning flash, blazing rebel, silk
stick-tights on the brisk cuffs of winter.

ELIZABETH KERLIKOWSKE

ON LEARNING OF THE ABUSED IRAQI PRISONERS

Spirit of Truth,
be with us today
as we wait in shame and dread
to learn of what our country has really done.

Spirit of Humanity,
bring us comfort.
May our tears be as the dew that glistens
on cobwebs that shimmer in the morning breeze.

Spirit of Justice,
help us find a way
to heal the wounds, to rebuild the holy shrines,
to make the world a safer, better place.

Spirit of Hope,
stay with us always.
May we recognize life's blessings
even while the storm rages.

Spirit of Love,
warm our hearts
with the smells of springtime.
Hold us close against the cold.

THERESA NOVAK

HELP ME SAY GOODBYE TO THE LEAVES

Grant me courage, Lord, to say goodbye
to the leaves,
to accept the turning.
I want to ignore the red and yellow
glimmers hidden among the greens—
proof that the seasons will,
as they always do,
change again.
The greens I draw energy from
will soon transform into brilliance,
then fall and disappear,
revealing long, black limbs against
grey November skies.
I will think of
times past,
people past,
mortality.
Give me courage, Lord,
to say goodbye.

LINDY CONROE

FRAGILITY/DIVINITY

We are fragile.
    We are not broken.
We are imperfect.
    We are not flawed.
We are curious.
    We are not confused.
We are vulnerable.
    We are not weak.
We are of this earth,
    and yet the divine lives in us.

When I feel as if I am going to break,
I am the most human.
When I embrace my fragility,
I let you into my imperfect world.

JILL-BETH SWEENEY SCHULTHEIS

THE WAVE DANCERS

This could be, I think, the ultimate meditation.
Lying in the huge silence, the roaring silence
separating them
from human discourse, how could they not,
in some way, encounter the Divine?

Out there, just beyond where the foam
breaks in the shallow wash
they lie in wait—bobbing like seals,
waiting for the big one,
panting to mount the huge high curl,
to ride its crest, conquer it like
a restive bronco.

Black-suited stick men,
they rise on the boards
when the swell feels right,
then spring to action, black arms for rudders,
and twisting, gyrating, swiveling,
ride the long, smooth downside
with terpsichorean grace—
or losing the dance's beat,
wipe out.

And onshore watching, I wonder at the mighty force
that brings them ever and ever back
to Poseidon's ballroom. The excitement
of the dance, the thrill of challenge,
the adrenaline rush of omnipresent danger?
All these and more, I'm sure.
And perhaps with all that, there is a peace
that settles on the soul when earth noises subside
in the roaring silence, creating a perfect solitude.

PEARL SAWYER

A SHOVEL FULL OF EARTH

A few shovel fulls
of earth
await humbly.
Dark brown as only
earth can be—
dug from the fragrant depths.

How shall we live
this life?
And isn't it
much grander
than this in the end?

No—the splendor
is right here,
in the dirt,
in the soil
that can grow
all we need
miraculously
and without fanfare.
With or without us,
it nourishes life
verdantly.

And so
I shall go, in time, as all
go

and greet
this sustaining
earth
with gratitude
and pray I
am worthy
and have served
Her well.

MELITTA HASLUND

A NEW DAY

Before dawn of the fall equinox, fourteen women
and I eagerly made our way in the dark by foot to a
Stone Age temple, Mnajdra. We had been on the
Mediterranean island of Malta for nine days, exploring numerous Neolithic temples dedicated to
Mother Earth still standing here. This morning's
excursion was the culmination of our trip, to watch
the rays of the rising sun illuminate the altar at the
fall equinox.

We had agreed beforehand to maintain silence at
least until sunrise. When we reached the top of the
hill above the temple we were told we had to wait
there, still quite a distance from the temple itself,
until closer to sunrise. My initial disappointment at
this news drained away as I stood looking around

me in the cool dimness before dawn. Only the sky was truly visible. A delicate quarter moon hung above surrounded by stars. I had barely focused on them when I saw a shooting star sweep in a graceful arc across the heavens. I felt blessed to be standing on a hill in Malta above an ancient temple on a lovely night with nothing to do but enjoy the beauty. I realized I seldom take more than a minute or two to enjoy the sky at home. As I waited there silently for nearly forty minutes, the sky gradually lightened, making the stars vanish. The moon became a tiny sliver and then it too disappeared. As the light grew stronger, the Mediterranean appeared below us near the temple, and birds began to sing loudly and insistently. By the time we were given permission to go down to the temple, I already felt fully nourished by beauty and gratitude.

We made our way down the walkway to the temple and found spots to stand where we could all see the altar. Still the sun did not appear over the horizon; I was surprised that sunrise was such a long and gradual process. Finally the long-awaited moment came, spilling thick, red-gold light onto the altar stone. A collective sigh whispered through the group of watchers. The Stone Age people's love and awe for the power and beauty of Mother Earth were movingly evident all around us. I was painfully aware of how far today's people have strayed from that reverent declaration of love.

Later, as I pondered the morning's experiences, I found it both funny and sad that all of us had traveled halfway across the world and stood waiting for more than an hour in great anticipation—to watch the sun rise, something that we could have done from our own doorways. Of course, we also came to be touched by the wonder of ancient people who erected huge temples aligned to the movement of the sun. But the temple builders weren't seeking to glorify their own prowess. They were celebrating the deeper wonder of the sun itself, making life possible by its return each day.

May we make space every day to remember what the ancients knew, what has been woven into the tissue of our hearts since the evolution of humankind—that the universe is a miraculous wonder to be celebrated and that a miracle that happens every day is no less a miracle.

ANNE PEEK

LADDERS

Two men walked casually, each with a wooden
    ladder
carried unceremoniously over the shoulder
as if the long and awkward burden
were no more than a sweatshirt,

or half-full bag, or at most a child of two
draped there for a few laughing moments.
But they went on from one job to another,
the bucket one held (and waved in careless gesture)
suggesting window-washers headed for the next pane.
The little puzzle of why they carried ladders
along the busy road was nothing to the beauty of
   their walking,
the unconscious grace
as they kept the long tools in parallel
(all the while talking, shrugging, chuckling)
and seemingly unaware of the swathe they cut
without harm to passers-by.
No pas-de-deux at center stage
could capture so lovingly
the rapture of ordinary life made remarkable
by mastery and unselfconscious pride.

JENNIFER BROOKS

THEY

They.

They're cutting down trees
and they're raising taxes.
They're making our children violent and fat.
They're blowing us up

and they're remaking bad decisions.
They're destroying the world
one by one.

They.
It's what we say,
hiding behind a word
full of blame and disassociation—
an ignorant, irresponsible nation.

But

they
do not exist.
There is only
we.

We cut down the trees
and We raise the taxes.
We make our children violent and fat.
We blow ourselves up
and We make bad decisions.
We destroy the world
as one.

We
are a world
community.
We
must take responsibility.

DANA DWINELL-YARDLEY

PEACE ON EARTH

Most nights it was much the same.
Sheep restless now and then,
but mostly still.
Wool heavy, tangled,
black shiny with mud of mid-day rain.
Rock-strewn, close-cropped earth
pebbled by the flock's hard leavings.
Sky sharp with stars,
a silent chorus above,
a grand and distant harmony.

Tough—as always—for hired hands.
Stay vigilant through tedious hours.
Be alert despite the cold
seeping in through hands and blankets,
each man and animal
breathing a gently rhythmic fog.

But this night more.
A light, was it?
A message, a call perhaps?

Be up and moving!
There is a chance
to go and see
and be a part of something—
some questing after peace,

some building of good will,
not just for some but for all.

Then risk flock and job and livelihood
for but a hope?
Set course by a beacon sure to dim with time?
Descend to gabbling, garrulous town,
perhaps to lose forever
the very peace that's sought?

Most nights it is the same.

JACK KING

WALKING THROUGH A SNOWSTORM

The densely falling snow
makes the world seem smaller somehow.
Normally expansive mountain vistas
are veiled by a finely woven curtain of white.
I am alone out here,
alone with the sound of my breath
and my boots crunching through the snow.
When I pause in my tracks,
all is silent
save the soft patter of snow on the brim of my hat
and the dark solitary cry of an unseen raven.
Alone, but not lonely.

When I circle back to retrace my steps,
I find that my footprints have already been filled in,
and I wonder if it is better to tread heavily in this
    world
and leave a long-lasting mark,
or to tread lightly.
I lean toward the latter.

TESS STARECHESKI

REFLECTION

Great blue heron,
tall solemn bird,
wades in the water,
wary and wise, slow to startle
or to rise. . . .
Now great wings open wide,
pushing off, pushing high—
long legs lifting, head leading
above the calm lake surface.
Then—sudden, surprising!—
riding to greet the real heron I see
the clear reflection of itself.
Shimmering wings respond to wings widespread,
watery body below grey, feathered breast
in moving, mirrored harmony.

Oh Great Spirit, so buoy me
that I too will spread my wings and try
to fly this fearlessly,
knowing that my silent cries
and surge of soul—like heron rise—
shall answer be.

CAROLINE BALDERSTON PARRY

UNITARIAN UNIVERSALIST
MEDITATION MANUALS

Unitarians and Universalists have been publishing
annual editions of prayer collections and meditation
manuals for 150 years. In 1841, the Unitarians broke
with their tradition of addressing only theological
topics and published *Short Prayers for the Morning and
Evening of Every Day in the Week, with Occasional Prayers
and Thanksgivings.* Over the years, the Unitarians
published many volumes of prayers, including
Theodore Parker's selections. In 1938, *Gaining a
Radiant Faith* by Henry H. Saunderson launched the
current tradition of an annual Lenten manual.

Several Universalist collections appeared in the early
nineteenth century. A comprehensive *Book of Prayers*
was published in 1839, featuring both public and pri-
vate devotions. During the late 1860s, the Universalist
Publishing House was founded to publish denomina-
tional materials. Like the Unitarians, the Universalists

published Lenten manuals, and in the 1950s they complemented this series with Advent manuals.

Since 1961, the year the Unitarians and the Universalists consolidated, the Lenten manual has evolved into a meditation manual, reflecting the theological diversity of the two denominations. Today the Unitarian Universalist Association meditation manuals include two styles of collections: poems or short prose pieces written by one author—usually a Unitarian Universalist minister— and anthologies of works by many authors.

2005   *Admire the Moon* Mary Wellemeyer
2004   *We Build Temples in the Heart* Patrick Murfin
         Consider the Lilies Stephen M. Shick
2003   *Walking Toward Morning* Victoria Safford
         How We Are Called Mary Benard and
               Kirstie Anderson, Editors
2002   *Instructions in Joy* Nancy Shaffer
         Roller-skating as a Spiritual Discipline
               Christopher Buice
2001   *This Piece of Eden* Vanessa Rush Southern
         Dancing in the Empty Spaces David O. Rankin
2000   *Glad to Be Human* Kaaren Anderson
         Out of the Ordinary Gordon B. McKeeman
1999   *The Rock of Ages at the Taj Mahal*
               Meg Barnhouse
         Morning Watch Barbara Pescan